# About the Author

George Gunn was born in Thurso, Caithness, where in 1996 he returned to live and work with the Grey Coast Theatre Company, of which he is the Artistic Director. He is well-known for his stage plays – the latest of which, *The Houses of the Sea,* was performed at the Dràma Na h-Alba Theatre Festival in Inverness. He has had seven collections of poems published, most recently *Winter Barley* (Chapman, 2006). In 2003 he received a Royal Literary Fund award and in 2006 a Scottish Arts Council Writer's Bursary.

# THE ATLANTIC FOREST

## George Gunn

TWO RAVENS
PRESS

Published by Two Ravens Press Ltd
Green Willow Croft
Rhiroy
Lochbroom
Ullapool
Ross-shire IV23 2SF

# www.tworavenspress.com

ISBN: 978-1-906120-26-9

British Library Cataloguing in Publication Data: a CIP record
for this book can be obtained from the British Library.

Designed and typeset in Sabon by Two Ravens Press.
Cover design by David Knowles and Sharon Blackie.

Printed on Forest Stewardship Council-accredited paper by
Biddles Ltd., King's Lynn, Norfolk.

**Mixed Sources**
Product group from well-managed
forests, controlled sources and
recycled wood or fiber
FSC   www.fsc.org  Cert no. TT-COC-002303
© 1996 Forest Stewardship Council

# Acknowledgements

Some of these poems have appeared in *Scotia Review, Poetry Scotland* and *Northwords*.

The author would like to thank the Scottish Arts Council for a Writer's Bursary and HI-Arts for a Development Award which made the writing of this book possible.

Also and especially to Joy Hendry for her constancy.

# Contents

| | |
|---|---|
| THE SOLUTION | 1 |
| THE NOSTALGIA WARS | 2 |
| AN ATLANTIC SPRING | 3 |
| AN ATLANTIC FOREST CLEARING | 5 |
| RED CAR | 6 |
| MOTH ON THE WINDOW | 7 |
| THE JULY MOON | 8 |
| MARS | 9 |
| MY GRANDFATHER OGUN | 10 |
| SAGA | 12 |
| SLIPPAGE | 14 |
| THE XMAS DAWN | 15 |
| THE BREATH OF LOKI | 17 |
| THE FOUNDLING | 25 |
| THE BEAR SKIN | 26 |
| A PRELUDE | 27 |
| OCCUPYING POWERS | 28 |
| TAPHONOMY | 29 |
| BEACH WALK | 32 |
| BARBARIANS | 33 |
| THE STRONGHOLD OF LIGHT | 34 |
| A BRIEF HISTORY OF OCCUPATION | 35 |
| A MESSAGE | 36 |
| FALLUJAH REQUIEM | 37 |
| JUST AS THE FULMAR SAID | 39 |
| THE PLAYWRIGHT LAMENTS | 40 |
| CAPTAIN ANON | 41 |
| NOVEMBER WAXWINGS | 42 |
| DUNNET KIRKYARD | 44 |
| A JOURNEY TO LYBSTER | 45 |
| HALFWITS UNDER SNOW | 46 |

| | |
|---|---|
| QUARRY | 48 |
| THANATOS | 49 |
| JULIAN ON DUNNET BEACH | 50 |
| THE LAST DAYS OF WINTER | 53 |
| BELIEF | 54 |
| POSTCARDS | 56 |
| THE ADDER'S CONFESSION | 57 |
| IT'S SPRING | 59 |
| THREE OBSERVATIONS ON THE COSMIC WHEEL | 60 |
| ROB DONN | 61 |
| IN THE SPRINGTIME OF EUROPE | 62 |
| IN DEFENCE OF POETRY | 64 |
| IN PIEROWALL KIRKYARD | 65 |
| FIRTH MUSIC | 66 |
| BLOOD FOG | 67 |
| ST ANDREW'S DAY | 68 |
| PENTECOST | 69 |
| THE MIGHTY ATLANTIC | 70 |
| BLUE | 73 |
| THE ATLANTIC FOREST | 75 |
| IN THE ATLANTIC FOREST | 76 |
| CODA | 84 |

# THE SOLUTION
*For PB*

We walked into a valkyrie of rain
'iceodrops' you said
we were washed in a May shower
of sandstone light
into the egg yolk of dunes
filling our footprints
with the sucking sound of razor fish
& the brine Atlantic sheen
which hung above the village
vinegared our noses with the iodine smell
of a hayturner & tractor oil
bread & india-rubber tyres
so fat & chevroned
they patterned the black earth
of the croft parks like peat-cut braid
the beach before us beckoning
the tongue of the tide licking at the bay
like an April calf at an empty milk pail
we walked wet to the widening sky
beneath our feet littered shells
lay random & unsettled like ideas
filleting our tiny fears
of the somehow absent presence of death
we walked weaving ourselves into meaning
leaving behind like a faint rainbow
our promise to the sea-lit sand
to never become a symptom
of the problem we mean to solve

1

# THE NOSTALGIA WARS

At night they fly across the townland
some seconds before their noise
the sky is forced down to touch the ground
the red winking war-light beneath the fuselage
flicks fear through the innocent stars

they poison silence
I would push them back
to a time when brown sails
flagged the Moray Firth
from coast to coast
consuming shoals of herring

I would wrap them in the quiet pathway
washed flat with human blood

these planes have broken the compact
our generation made with time
we will not cripple the Spring blossom
nor slaughter the gambolling lamb
or point too early at the smouldering fire

I would catch them in my hand
& still the conflicting heart

# AN ATLANTIC SPRING

May is made for growing
the green hair of breather corn
the rain-listening elephant ear of rhubarb
light opens night's cage
& signals the seabirds to the cliff ledges
or to burrow like puffins into the peat lip
of clett or sea-stac

on the far shore of three thousand miles
the frigate bird callipers an ancient V
compassing gulf & river delta
for Carib & Amazonian
before Columbus & Cortez

in Caithness fulmars figure eight
close to the sandstone palate of Dunnet Head
the sharp Pentland air sifts through
the chalk blue fimbriate of their feathers
the lengthening day pours into their eyes

I stand on the edge of the Easter geo
beside the stark Stevenson lighthouse
feet firmly on the stone bow
of the ship of Scotland
"North" I cry "take me North
to that other Atlantic forest
before another decade of rock
erodes this poor certainty"

my hands reach out for time before I do
a few freckles of age above the knuckle
the epic confetti of Calliope

# AN ATLANTIC FOREST CLEARING

October gloves the scented harvest passing
of September's barley fields ploughed
into the butcher meat shawl of earth
which shoulders Dunnet Head
from Duncansby to Olrig Hill
now the fingers of Winter slide
the smell of baking bread & poppy seed
down into the ice-barn of dreaming
where seasons melt & form
into organisation's white passion
that will both freeze & burn
the calendars of disjointed days
into the patterns of history
that lap both sides of the ocean

2

Keeking Kierkegaard called the swirling
pointlessness of the universe "God"
the boy sees the same starry milk above him
& calls it Saturday night
down here on the godless roads
which embrace the absurd
& roll it into a bible
for it is a short free kick
to 1919 & the sea of Kilmarnock bunnets
with the Red Flag flying over George Square
& the beauty of our refusal
stolen by those who inhaled handcuffs
in the hungry years of meaning
when the peace-time army blocked the streets

# RED CAR

Silent as a lie
the truth congregates
around Thurso
like fish

the man gets out of the red car
which would buy
the council house
he stands in front of

the Summer is a grey lump
the radio noise
which pours out of his car
like concrete

tells us that his department
has no respect
for any thing
including itself

what happens here
is that we wrap up the future
in a gas
they call song

which no one on the north coast
has ever heard of
searching for rats
in this red car

in the ripping up of my heart
in this slow swim

# MOTH ON THE WINDOW

White as paper
an eyelid of moth
hangs on the window
like a message
of what you are seeing
although you are not here
the moth holds the traces
of you in the ink
of its wings
so now I see you
in this letter of a moth
on this cinema of a window

# THE JULY MOON

The moon is a golden lamp
the moon is a Grimbister cheese
the moon is the eye of a salmon
the moon the moon the moon
in July

its light throws open the trapdoors
to where the day still is hidden
where the bark tongue blackens further
from the glove of intrusive headlights
the moonlight is an escape
from the desperate wisdom
of fear & jealous hands
joining land to sea
with heather ropes
ropes of sand and moonlight
tying time to the rock of history
but unlike the moon
they cannot move
cannot climb & have no orbit
save for the tarry triangle of corners
which pass for arguments about rain
the moon is rich
in its ever balancing treasury of heaven
the great coin of gravity
bleeding music from the night

# MARS
*For Colin MacKay 1951 – 2003*

I long for the berries to ripen
for their redness to fall
into the opening ground
like solid blood
so young in their age
forests should grow from them
the rowans of a fresher & deeper hue
so needed upon the earth
this coming of age
this possible beauty
so September sings
hidden in the nervous
puckered lips of Autumn
whispering into the empty space
above in the true black
south eastern sky
Mars is an orange dot
as the pink dawn pours
across the morning horizon
a pale phoenix
at home in the rowan berries
unfulfilled pulse
where all are so contained
this not quite red
this not quite anything
this soft arrival
disguised as departure
coated in the language of madmen
& insomniac rooks

# MY GRANDFATHER OGUN
*The Blacksmith*

Tall, leaning forward like a pine in the wind
he strode to the smiddy
smoke streaming from his pipe like an engine
all day he worked thinking

At night as he lay beneath the Caithness sky
he stretched out like the Strath of Kildonan
his dream a cradle of fire
his hands constantly searching
for hammer, tongs & cutting torch
he formed the earth
with the skill of a blacksmith
he butchered his own meat
with tender metal feathers
as sharp as adder fangs

His smiddy was a tool-stacked temple
tins of washers and drill bits
lathes, welding gear & vices
all set in a pattern
to engineer his impulse
on the altar of the anvil
before the fertile forge of his creation

When he awoke the fire was fresh
with flickering orange music
as when rebellion turns into revolution
he will dress in black

with a red scarf around his neck
he will caress the bellows into thunder
but will still hold the lamb
an iron bracelet on his wrist

My grandfather, Ogun, raises his arm
& the birds of liberty fly around his hammer
his Northern smiddy is full now
with the dancing blacksmith's noise
of peace, sweat & struggle

# SAGA

In a field of frozen haystacks
blue light from a northern moon
shines down
upon grey moving figures

casting shadows
on the silver ground
all are caught in history's ambush
everyone is undone by time

the moon sails across
the indigo sea of the night
the haystacks shiver
as the figures struggle

reddening the frost
of the petrified harvest
he strives to be free for her
she sits & longs for him

so the moon conducts this dance
beneath the glacier
on the edge of the ocean
in such a setting

there can be no conclusion
the ice will release
the buried colours of their action
& set in motion

the desire to complete
that which can never be completed
in a field of frozen haystacks
beneath a Northern moon

# SLIPPAGE

Six fishermen pass coiled ropes
to each other along the deck
getting ready for the ocean

meanwhile the tide is rising
the mooring lines are slackening

soon they will be adrift
preparing for their journey
which unbeknown to them
has already begun

# THE XMAS DAWN

The Xmas dawn is a thin blue
smiling child
with snow in her hair
& the smoke of night
in her sleepy eyes
emerging like a salmon
by a black rock
from an awkward sea
a flowering of light
a coming back from the dead
a morning of flowers & blood
when dreams are hanging
like a fresh fish
over a peat fire in Winter

the Xmas dawn

2

The morning is a silver wheel
driven by the bird-silent memory
of last night's anxious frost

A white cat plays beneath
the black branch of the horizon
her swiping & flicking tail
the two searching hands of a momentary clock

The yellow dustcart fills the Northern silence
with the organised noise of the corporate machine
bins are emptied like heads of dreams
& the morning has been rolled
east along the road
by these significant chances
it opens now in the child's hands

as the Messiah chases Venus home

3

The orange sky is a grey cloud lit
by starlight beyond the grey
the slate horizon holds the watercolours
of the rising day
in yellows, thin blues & gentle browns

All this light passes through the prism of a life
lived by running ahead of the darkness
knowing that the green fields beneath the feet
support a dream
that human organisation is like a tree
whose leaves if they fall upon the head
will stun with the iron of their false promises

now these leaves melt into the sun
as the young & hungry world emerges
from the quarry of the night

blood from a flagstone Bethlehem

# THE BREATH OF LOKI
*For RAJ*

The sky is emptying itself
the horizon pushes up
to absorb the coming cold
for a week it has rained
& now the river's heart is full
the sea off the coastline is brown
ships like ages pass through blood
& memory is the coming ice
driven south by Loki's breath
across the unbelieving ocean
perhaps we will be changed forever
& will never notice that 'perhaps'
that time has already iced over
in the triumph of the joking hungry god

for like Sappho & Catulus
this age has no biography
only fragments of verse
to tell of what it was
to cut into the stone heart of the state
its epitaph


2


The clouds do not go empty to their grave
they do not die but drift
like living ghosts across the sky
to life's beginning & the perfection

of their own work
where old is new & boundaries & limits
are transgressed continually
their destruction is their source
& so beginning close up again
in this vast Caithness sky
& the time is coming like the storm
when all that has risen up
over & through the hopes of generations
will lie like straw on a Winter field

Those who have been so deceived
tell of their aspirations
in the semaphore of the rain
& those who reinterpret them
sign arrogance as their name
on the underbelly of the cloud

3

The ground is divided between the few
who the many have to pay
in order for the few to maintain their scorn
who lacking the vision of even a forecast
cannot see how it soon will be
for them as the tide rises
& threatens to cover over
their subsidy, their privilege, their riches
which they would increase
if only they could
Time will not say

when they can expect the levelling sea
it only sings "I have to do it & I will"
then did

The circling Atlantic sends down
the swirling darkness of her trickster's art
the moment awaits itself
above where the tides touch
is mere illusion
when the old return to youth

4

So it comes, the grey blue sea
is torn to towering ribbons
as the north wind cuts hard
into the squat sea-facing town
Out beyond the headland
a volcano of angry promise
threatens the firth, the cliffs, the fields
the breath of Loki has blown
& the beach is gone where once Hector stood
waiting for another storm
The voices of the dead howl onto the shore
from the raging boiling sea
from the place destruction forged
the familiar designs of fear

So it comes, the hard concentrating imagination
snapping like midnight frost beside the river
she will walk there, the one whose face

has witnessed what it wears
no shield can protect her now
everything is exposed

5

Still sleeps the snow
like the secret in a shell put to the ear
the ghostly sound of the sea
will shake its hair
like a waking girl
caught up in the dream tangle
of the awkward driven surf
& put ice in the grey blanket
which covers her shoulders
as she turns into Duncansby Stacks
guarding the ground for seabirds
for it is the morning now
the earth must wait
for the warming furrow of the plough

No one speaks, memory lies under the snow
in the iron gallery of silence
portraits of versions of shadows
hang from the robbing eyes of rooks
In limps Oedipus, blind & alone
Antigone gone

6

The Moon lies on her back
she is being dragged through the stars
by an eager Venus
like a shining sledge
eventually both are consumed
by the vast black adder of the night
so that night's promise could be no more
Listen, hear the hooves of the new centurions
drumming on the skulls
a percussion of a mud-tradition
of potatoes, turnips & hayfields
of the Moon in the frozen earth
the snow in tiny revolutions
the light in the sleepless seeds

The night is an orchestra of hands
the Moon is an absence of generals
Venus is a sorrow of badges
the snow is the anxious tapping
on the closed library door
white adders are singing the anthems of engines

7

Horses chased them down the streets
of broken Warsaw in 1944
or Hatfield in 1984
or here where a small king's vanity
cheapens the landscape of the voice

Soon moss will grow on the monuments
erected to fresh ideas
& this night which feels like the caress
of a blizzard of truncheons
will seem pleasant then
in that time not far off
down the ruined avenues
where shoes are abandoned
beside battered pianos & dropped membership cards


The ice will cover Dunnet Head
Tiresias, our new cartographer
has changed his mind & now charts
glaciers from Holborn to Hoy
paints Pegasus & Beaucephalus
in the margins of his new map

8

The blizzard has us tight
grey smoke swirling around towers
Pasternak at Peredelkino cutting wood
for the infernally tricky stove
Whiteout & everything vanishes
Caithness Russia the Dunbar Hospital
beneath this Arctic Medusa
this consummate translation turning
the seabed-north of fossils & ditches
into the savage pure poetry
of a beautiful extreme

at home around our throats choking
or searching out its own memorable phrases
from our sturdy grammar of brochs & geos


What we knew once we have lost now
it forms in snow crystals upon the window
like the skin of an ice leopard
dreamed up by Ovid as he wanders
through the blizzard in search of Odessa
the snow drifts over his footprints again

9


Snorri Sturluson sat & watched the hailstones fall
the wind ripping itself against the mouth of the cave
he pulled the Icelandic shawl around him
like paper meat & laughed
at Loki's attempt to set him here
stormbound on a small island
the storm laughed back
hailstones bouncing like discarded teeth
but laughing still, like judges
after justice, after the ripping wind
has caught the offending file
sending it heavenward or into hyperspace
laughing at fish farms, wind turbines, bridges
at Diogenes rolling in his barrel

stones stuffed in his mouth
so that the senate can sit & enquire into itself
on how perfect it has become
roasting monkeys on a spit
immortal in the immaculate prose
of a history writing itself in sand

10

The storm has gone leaving its tendrils
in the rock pool of the sky
Loki the mischief-maker squats down
at the Western side of the sea-grey firth
he washes his hair in the dreaming surf
high above him a falcon swoops
cutting shapes from the snow-salt air
he sits down upon the headland, his task done
all the sacrificial lambs have risen up
the seekers of eternal youth have settled
for the worm-eyed apples of their own
camera-less demise, their impossible demands
on the green fields of their lives
Loki brushes his hair with the comb of continents

You who will walk away from the moment
when your mask meets your nerve
may see golden patterns
emerging like gruesome flowers
from the body of the fallen world
All Loki sees is apples

# THE FOUNDLING

I am the Spring lamb
a late Winter offering
my own thief

2

He said, what we do is
we gather up everything
because we believe in nothing
experience everything
giving nothing
& stand aside
like empty statues
seeking destruction
in our own shadow
this is our wisdom
& always out of reach
opening as it shuts
a story of wealth
for the wretched

3

The world can see
can we see the world?

## THE BEAR SKIN
*For PB at 44*

He grabs the new skin she gave him
& quickly slips it on
sidles over to the corner & sits
stroking its brown reassurance
in a methuselah of memories
Outside the sky is moonless
freezing in expanding time
The cosmos gathers round
& looks down
He shuffles outside
& looks up
he reaches for various planets & stars
rubs them into the bristling grey-haired fur
& decides to shine

# A PRELUDE

The grey ships of Winter still sail south
& frozen February reaches her end
flagstone dykes lean & hug the snow
a solitary crow circles through the drift
trying to entice the threatening sun
to brighten up the blue behind the Arctic smoke
everything is shivering on this psalmless Sunday

From the sea comes the storm of flame & frost & snow
So act out the gods as if Caithness were a stage
to set the Orkneying Saga
but things below are nervous
the fabric's being unstitched
crofts are being bought for Summer houses
ruins change hands for forty grand
folk sleep in boats & caravans
the civic shirt is hanging by the bed
the fishing fleet is decommissioned
the glass factory in receivership
the atomic station no longer lit by delight
headlights beam across the starless night
three Winters meet on Dunnet Head

The local elect sip their silent whisky
the press dance through a geography of ghosts
the population vote with their absent young
stamp their feet through the insistent weather
saying to themselves as much as one another
"We freeze here as easily as we melt
the wind cuts through more than the mortgage rate"

# OCCUPYING POWERS

All morning for fifty years
they have ripped the sky to thunder
& still they come the screaming Yanks
ghost for ghost & breath for breath
the bleeding clouds are spoken for
making safe the space for noise
by accommodating yet another noise

The blue sea of Spring is not tolerant
some thousand feet below as free as Oedipus
they manoeuvre & track out of the Sun
searching for the enemy
which locates behind their eyes
a missile path across the Firth
to level an imaginary plague-ridden city

I will count them in & warm my hands
at the bonfire of shadows & vapour trails
watching dogs arch in the half-light
to shit themselves out of their own arse

# TAPHONOMY

*Taphonomy is the study of what survives in archaeology,
principally art objects, in relation to time, nature and
human activity.*

In East Anglia Cromwell cut his way out
of a landscape described by New Romantic TV presenters
as "uncompromising"
My recollection of all that fear is of flat
featureless horizon-hugging fields
& of being lost because I could never calculate
where this reclaimed geometry had set the sea
Amongst such beautiful confusion
survival is the eternity of a dragonfly
& I can only marvel like a beheaded statue
that such a place could produce puritan certainty
Deep in England's reed beds
I have never felt so wrong
or so uncertain


2


The explosion of Vesuvius in 79 AD killed Pliny the Elder
as Pompeii & Herculaneum disappeared under a
                                        pyroclastic cloud
witnessed by Pliny the Younger
in a perfect yet gruesome symmetry
of entrances & exits much as the Himalayas & the Andes
are lifted up in a slow collision of continents
they are ground down by rain & ice
granite oozes from the earth to harden into obdurate stone

over time feldspar becomes clay
quartz turns to sand & trickles down rivers & burns
to build fertile flood plains & beautiful beaches
that one day will become sandstone uplands
to signify Baltica Gondwana Pangea
all lost beneath the ancient sea of Tethys

3

What survives is a temporary present
at the rate of a growing fingernail continents creep
everything is a tidemark of frozen music
One Summer on Innismore
enjoying the hundred miles of drystone walls
I heard a strange & happy singing
coming from nowhere I could see
suddenly on a ledge below my feet
buck-naked & bearded under a green hat
was a man painting the grey Atlantic slabs of Aran's cliffs
onto his patient easel
he waved his brush at me as if to include me in
or catch a bit more sun singing all the while
to make the world closer & unfolding like the rocks an
                                                    open secret

4

Trawling through the handiest metamorphoses
they can strap to their wings, our glorious leaders fly
with the aerial tumbrels of the occasional truth
& the necessary inadvertent lie

posted out in the enveloping air
their arms stretched to the very margins of chaos
finding only the nameless law of separation
which no one had thought of before
rolled into a ball
so that each approach is the same into this happy heaven
this hanging substanceless search
for Boreas & the law of graves
which questions what has or what has not survived
& what has or what has not been discovered

# BEACH WALK
*Five Years On*

Fingers emerge from beneath the sand
knuckles taut in an ampersand
faces formed by the fleeing tide
the nights grow light
the kings collide
this is no beach for you tonight
the tongueless sea will not reply
they search for you & use your eye
horizons cut across the sky
voices weapon up the wind
the skin falls off & will never end
the crabs are children of the moon
the somewhere sergeant will see you soon
all of this you say you understand

between Babylon & Sutherland

# BARBARIANS

Cavafy wrote of "expecting the barbarians"
who never came because
there were no barbarians any more
The Emperor twirled his jewelled cane
in expectation of the end
but that was 1950
& these are the early years of a new century
& the tragedy Cavafy feared
is a comedy we must now live
if life is possible when fresh air is rationed
It is the Emperor who approaches the city
a barbarian from his helmet to his boots
his tanks stretch from the suburbs to the border
his airforce fills the sky

# THE STRONGHOLD OF LIGHT
*For Willie Wilson*

The sky folds north
in a thousand shades of grey
the light is caught by the rain
& stored in the flagstones

so we build, each day
another stone washed by the sea
all our desires a harvest
of tides, quarrying & weather

all put, one upon the other
until they fuse as if fired
by both defender & attacker
across the rolling eyeline of Caithness

this is not the landscape for strongholds
here we catch ourselves like silver in the rain

# A BRIEF HISTORY OF OCCUPATION

The cynicism of Camelot
chasing a dream
to invent a history
every conqueror's necessity
from William to the House of Hanover
burying their weapons at our sacred sites
building their strongholds over our fields

# A MESSAGE
*For Atefeh Rajabi 1988 – 2004*

The red eyes of the rowans
drop out of the Highlands
like tears of blood
the blue of Loch Fleet
is their Autumn towel
how well the world is
when humans are absent
the fireweed along the banks in Tain
is like candyfloss
the green birches huddle
in happy conversation
the harvest settles down
upon the straths & ripens
our journey then is long

The fields will evaporate in time
all the sunlight sweeps
the Summer up into a bale
& the hills in the west
will gather up their trust
& store it in the rocks & scree
I will not see you in the morning
my friend
I will be on the other side
of the ocean
I only say this as one
who has loved you well
the Moray Firth is there for all time
& everything eventually is human

# FALLUJAH REQUIEM

Sitting in a booth in Johnny Foxes it begins
women discuss Mozart's "Requiem"
in Inverness in the rain
as the world folds into its third quarter
when the moon is halved
& swivels on her back
the tide hugs the dunes on Dunnet Beach
September shakes her hair
as the river runs pure
& everybody is listening
to the nervous music
which the river has pressed like grapes
& pours down like green wine
from the western mountains

When the earth breathes like this
the rain dries itself
& the low yellow sunlight
spreads the devalued currency
of desire over the buildings
the trees are coated in honey
& the unfinished list of our crimes
flies & sticks to the branches
like a summons of spit
suddenly the conversation of the women
is the clicking of computer games
how will you survive this pathetic world
when your energy pack runs out
& everything is absurd like a requiem?

I will enter the room & ask: where do you look
is it across the vast familiar bog
or is it over the well-thumbed pages of history?
All we find in either is ourselves
so where do we look instead?
I have the famous sea around me
it is like some magnificent dreaming carpet
the orchestra – can you hear them? – is silent
you brought it with you
they are stacked up in the back of your head
can you see Morven from there
how are the midges, the silence?
If we are anything we are landscape & music
painted brown & flowing like Kildonan

Did you see the green birches by the river
did you hear their footsteps there
running through the trees, the ferns
they are ghosts leaping across burns
do you not look, must I plead with you
can you not hear this requiem?
The deer hear them, the hare, the eagle
they smell the age-heavy rattling
which is the music which is not there
is there isn't there is
they see it in the silent anxiety which is time
are you still looking or hearing?
For this is how we celebrate
the quiet nature of destruction & it is over

# JUST AS THE FULMAR SAID

I care little for the regiments of the dead
although soon enough I will join them
but let them keep their military rows
their tidy quilt patches of memory & grief
eternity needs no walls
let me dance with my sister flame
into the ashes of the night
there I will be with those
who move forever towards the light
where the timeless sandstone
nuzzles into the sea
here I ran upon Dwarick Head
so now as in the past
scatter me, just as the fulmar said

Bury me not where nothing grows
& never blows the wind
turning every daylong page
a year in the making
then in an instant is gone the age
& all remain to savour simply nothing
I will free you of that
so you can read Dunnet Bay
as if the sea were freshly rhymed
with all the colours painted new
& never is unknown
where fish & seals & seabirds fly
through the flaming fingers of a life
lived beneath these cliffs of blood, this sky

# THE PLAYWRIGHT LAMENTS

I'm losing my actors to the call centres
I see them in bars on Saturday night
they're drunk from fear
& the sudden rush of money
but the poems are silent
in the mouths of the gods
& I can't hear anyone laughing
not as the lights go out
& the audience grows nervous
the man in the suit in the neon room
said there were too many of us
that he wanted to do more with less
well less is winning
in the final scene where there is nothing

# CAPTAIN ANON

*In memoriam The Ghillie Mhor*
*Hamish Henderson 1919 – 2002*
*on D–Day 2004*

Is being dead anonymous enough for you
now that the "D–Day Dodgers"
has been reported in the press
to have been written "by soldiers"?
I sit here in Inverness where the music
is traditional Scottish fiddle
I know that without you the Summer
will still be the Summer
but they wouldn't be playing this slow air
It is sixty years since you wrote that song
in reply to Nancy Astor
& the world seems unable to learn
from your struggle for peace
I know only one thing:
we own nothing
can never acquire it
should never aspire to it
What is anything worth
that innocents must die for it?
The east coast of Caithness
lay like a green slate this morning
& all the authorship of the world was there
for you who ran ashore singing
armed with our history
& a thirst for humanity
that nothing would relieve
I will walk out with you tonight
into the applause of silence

# NOVEMBER WAXWINGS

A signal of waxwings migrated south from Norway
on day one & brought the north
& Winter with them
they thought us safer somehow milder
this their first seasonal sojourn south
they did not see our darkening sea-lochs
our false-bridged kyles
our timber-tight firths
our storm-slapped islands
night came from Norway then
with these innocent birds
harbingers, soft bells of feather
how they beat about our Scottish rock
peeling off Europe like fear

On the second day the lights went out
as from across the Atlantic we saw the signs
that Grendel had roamed the middle lands
had ploughed the Ohio red
from Boston to San Bernardino
the Bluecoats held Moses prisoner in Des Moines
& the hymns flowed like rivers
to bury in flood those who hoped
across the broad puritan plain
of this November's tragic beginning
as America reformed again
& like the dolls in Yeats lay
we turned our faces to the wall
this was only the second day

Suddenly the trees look very bare
Winter swims in under the cold bark
the isolated leaves return
to the kingdom of the wind
the sky is as pale as porcelain
the weight of the coming Winter
pushes down upon the beliefless parks
the bald plough cuts its silence in a shed
& the morning grows dark
with the slow speed of an abandoned idea
& the November dawn has Winter's yellow light
so brief so fine & somehow easily gone
so that we must repeat our fear
& invade ourselves

They blossom on berries these birds
brightly coloured like small cockatoos
exotic in our russet daylight
they land like a flurry of clowns
on our hillsides & exhausted gardens
this ground we have wrestled from time
given the value of blood
named in the honesty of recognition
put song into & extracted music from
this place where the dead grow
like silver birch trees like the sullen ash
they have come here into our trust
refugees aliens escapologists troubadours
optimists ghosts survivors saviours

Let us tell it in Gath in this month of rubble

# DUNNET KIRKYARD

The Norwegian church sits in a dune-lap of bones
schooners are sketched onto the pew lip
the flagstone tables in the hotel car park
seem to us like the sacrificial site
for something or other
in the bay the sea tears itself up like paper
bookended between a sandstone list of psalms
chiselled into every wall
here we can read of women who died young
in childbirth
of men who gulped the decreasing sea
of various oceans
women who lived long enough
to kiss the silver cup of Jacob
all here in this ceilidh of death
behind this universe of dry-stone
circling around the bay like geese
known to me everyone
by their touch

# A JOURNEY TO LYBSTER
*For Andy Thorburn*

The Winter sun struggles free of night
the Moray Firth drinks the grey light
the hollow churches stand naked on the coast
the winding road itself is lost
the fields are frozen to the earth
we have forgotten what we are worth
the distant headland cuts into the sea
the graveyard sits walled up & free
the mountain's harbour to the south
the coastline opens up its mouth
& sings of ruined crofts & tattered flags
on the road from fish to rags
the lighthouse beam our only boast
for all who love this grey coast

# HALFWITS UNDER SNOW
*They Say*

They say there has been no poetry written
about the war in the land of Iraq
yet I still hear the sound of a Celtic drum
from Altimarlich to Strath Naver
it beats in the peoples' blood
in the Winter snow and the Summer sun
as in Iraq the dead feed the ground
our Celtic drum beats out in Iraq
a military radio on its back
They say there has been no poetry written
about the war in the land of Iraq
yet still I hear the sound
of the people coming out of the ground
the rest is ear-kissing argument

2

They say the theatre in Scotland is thriving
& of its work we should be proud
but I see nothing but another voice
swallowing that of our own
& like the "Scottish" regiments
the commander's pukka language
snapping us into line
What I would do if I could (if I could make it)
so that propaganda is nothing (except a *fleur de mal*)
& say that Scottish theatre as yet does not exist
that we are occupied by the consuls

of the ruling powers & our writers
are in their prison & their shadows
walk across the stage of our capital

# QUARRY

A gull catches the low December Sun
& turns orange
Snow sits over Caithness
like uranium
the lemon slice moon
is painted onto the blue
Night is falling
the Sun will go down
everything is freezing
how beautiful is an issue
the moon is growing
people litter this landscape with their greed
Somewhere in Caithness there is a theatre
it is underground

# THANATOS

The December tide dragged the dunes
down to the foam-hiss
& the light thinned out over Olrig Hill
as we walked scarfwarm & coat-tied
through the brine-packed gloaming
towards the Yol-lit lights of Dunnet
gentle in its open palm of parks & roofs
east of the flowing Pentland Firth
& Dwarick's red-rocked head
Suddenly out of the smooring fireglow
of the coming night
thousands upon thousands of ratcheting rooks
as black as aching they feathered the sky
with their tattered uniform of temper

# JULIAN ON DUNNET BEACH

The sheep lay still & embedded as the sand
it now danced with its limbs four strange
right angles the tide had some twenty times
re-arranged since the great storm swept it
from its headland grazing to lie here
a fleece of bones & a head
Julian walked on the ghosts of slaughter
following him across the beach
past the one episode that was not of his hand
"This is the perfect cathedral for the guilty"
he thought as he watched the relentless surf
harbour its own ghosts of the recent storms
"I will cross more than from Dunnet to Olrig"
as the North Arctic beams flashed
upwards in the freezing Winter sky
he stopped & looked & was taken back
to the Dunnet Kirk where he killed his first mouse
a teardrop of blood on the flagstone
how this led to the pigeon he shot
with his Xmas air-rifle
how it lay & twitched on a drystone ivy wall
how he had to wring its neck
as sex entered him like an adder
then there were the rabbits hens turkeys
ducks & geese of every measure
foxes out on The Links & on Dunnet Head
there were the deer in Dunnet forest
everything that moved he claimed their blood
until one morning he arose & went out

& filled the world with slaughter
so that every blade of grass & clump of heather
turned red & every fir tree dripped blood
Dwarick Head turned crimson
as did the dubh lochs
& all the animals on the northern coast
lay dead with its frenzy
& the heart of the Sun burst
into a thunderstorm of blood
as he lay down & wept
here on this beach
the blood-red dunes behind him
like the grateful pillows of death
so then Julian slept with his eyes wide open
sweat sliding off him into the butchered sand
then after a healing time he awakens
& sees the carnage of his singular war
& vows to wander the beach
which is the world
until he can understand what he has done
but because of the blood
the beach is a thousand miles long
& as he wanders the blood-fuelled Sun
burns his hair so that it catches fire
& the pitiless North wind
freezes his arms & legs
so that he cannot move
but must stand as an icy human candle
so he dreams of all the animals in the world
& how they have fallen
to stones & arrows & guns

how they swirl above his head
a flotilla of innocence & anger
so that his desire spills into the sand
& he knows he himself must go
so he stops his passionless wandering
beside the dead sheep on Dunnet Beach
& he knows what he must do
"You will be my ferryman to the end of the world"
he tells the sheep who says nothing
so Julian lies down in the decaying sand
beside the carcass of the sheep
& caresses it & kisses its mouth
& sleeps with the only animal he has not killed
as another storm rages in from the West
the sky grows black & the ocean boils
& sweeps the beach as is its desire
& when it is spent & the morning comes
not a trace of the sheep or Julian
can anyone who is looking find
under a blue sky & a yellow Sun
on Dunnet Beach where the white surf beats

# THE LAST DAYS OF WINTER

The copper birches' ancient fire
floods the river banks
& cracks from frost
as the morning moves
up into the soft orange light
hearthed low & east
in the mouth of the strath
as Kildonan welcomes
her people back
in the last days of Winter

# BELIEF
*For PB on her forty-fifth birthday*

The golden sun lies next
to the silver mountains
a dark blue storm
smokes over the Moray Firth
the cliff road is grey from frost
as I slide down the east coast
towards you

What is this landscape but freedom?
Littered along its flagstone lid
are the ruined crofts of those
who went to fight for it
among the mud & lies of Flanders
their widows emigrated
to find it in the rock boulevards of America
& their children drove Model-Ts
far out into the desert
to watch the Sun sinking over the West
searching for it

The wild geese fly out to sea
in an arrowhead of belief
the salt air of Winter in their down
the voices of children singing
softly beneath the beat of their wings

All I know is that wisdom comes from work
in our intent & in our name
we place our dream
where power cannot affect us
resisting here on the margins
of someone else's map

All this swims from your eyes
into the lochan of morning
telling me as if I needed to know
there is no evidence to be crushed
in the fist of belief
like a flicker of sunlight
over ice

# POSTCARDS
*after Pasternak*

How lonely is the child who is lost
in a shrinking age?
I hold the postcards of love in my hand
have held them for fifty years
from one who lies now beside the river
like a shadow under a cloud
she gave them to me freely
& I pass them onto another
equally busy in the pictures of life
now she sends them back to me
like the breath that passes between us
like the weather rolling in off the Atlantic

Those who strive to organise restriction
cannot hold back such messages
they will bleed the future by the their butcheries
& call Spring pleasant in the Winter snow
but the child who plays in the garden
found in our sleeping selves
will call to you & bid you join in
as freely as these images & notes
of journeys that meant we were separate
only in distance which we can easily cover
with the skin we ink our words upon
the paper & lips of our time

# THE ADDER'S CONFESSION

The adder comes out to soak up the sunlight
rare they are & beautiful
Mhic Ivor or *nathair* of the hill
April brings them to the eye
they whisper to the budding bracken
"Rise, rise my friends & ship me to October"

So in rows like urinals the Cardinals stand
muttering liturgies in the dead languages
of the Roman Emperor's vanity
in a wooden box the old boy lies
decked out on a stretcher
in a yellow square
soon everyone will tire
of this ridiculous grief
& the Norwegian rabbi
they always posted as missing
will return to Dwarick Head
& lie down with the adder
under the democratic Sun

I write this from the front seat
of an abandoned Ford Sierra
by the side of a tattie field in Easter Ross
my name is Paul
but before the rush of blood
my victims called me Saul
how strange the world seems to me now
this adder I hold in my hand

is the only language I understand
I feel the Sun dip into my zig zags
I feel reborn
I am the venom under the Bishop's mitre
I am the Cardinal's red fang
I am Jesus the serpent
the snake of God

# IT'S SPRING

A glorious sunlight on this green strath
the glacier-dropped rocks sit like teeth
in the open mouth of a rich liar
all things conspire to draw us on
the spine of the river is blue
the birch moustache its bank in silver
deer dart like promises
across open boggy ground
Some hours on the morning is still new
above the strath the moon persists like a yellow ghost
the kirk squats like a stone midwife
surrounded by the advent calendar of the dead
a heron ascends in prehistoric flight
smelling the salt thirsty sea, low & itching to the east

new lambs eye the casual violent gulls
expertly pin-pointing nowhere
further south leaves broaden & hold the air

# THREE OBSERVATIONS ON THE COSMIC WHEEL

A shell for putting things in
a scallop
a knife
your tongue
yourself

The landscape offers up its beauty freely
we must never demand it

An old woman picks up her dog's shit
in the eternal urban ritual
of walking
the dog shits in the same place
every day
inhabiting its own nightmare
of excrement & history

(as I write this the same woman appears
with the same dog
the same shitting ritual)

The landscape offers up its beauty freely
even to this Hecuba

# ROB DONN
*1714 – 1777*

A hand
a ship
a salmon
a deer
the symbols of the Mackay bárdacht
chiselled into Bal na Keil
kirk altar in 1619
long before you drove your cattle
down to Falkirk and Crieff
Rob Donn
to learn news of The Pretender
or the new German king
who like you could not speak English
bard of Strathnaver
you lie outside with your wife
& all my many grandmothers
across the kyle in Durness
I draw what I can from these stones
from 1777 to now
in 2008
I walk between the wars

# IN THE SPRINGTIME OF EUROPE

The mist off the sea has stalled
from Ullapool to Kinlochbervie
the mountains are drying out
& the grey landscape lifts May
to three thousand feet & leaves it there
like a box in a loft
but who exactly is forgetting here
not the raven over Bheinn Hope
flying like a black arrow
from the bow of the wind
not the Highland Council road engineers
cellotaping strips of tarmac across Sutherland
so that the German & Dutch tourists
can ignore the passing places more forcefully
& the English can learn to wave
as they tow their caravans across the horizon
to congregate beneath the far Western ocean
with the liquid ease of conquerors
no-one forgets because memory laughs
both on the wing & under the wheel
because the cliffs wear the waves like blinking eyelids
& all the houses are stone suitcases
in the nervous hands of history's emigrants
so alone & empty they look
as they have abandoned roofs & doors
in their anxious queuing to escape
so forlorn in their foundation-loosening moment
that they must be welcomed back
so that they can change colour & language

so that they can eat hummus instead of brose
& dance for Estonia instead of America
& remember Bratislava by the shores of Bal na Keil
for we are in the springtime of Europe
& the morning is opening out

# IN DEFENCE OF POETRY
*In Memoriam Giolla Brighde Mac Con Midhe*
*circa 1240 – 1280*

The slate grey eternity of the new priests
comes with their melting seals of certainty

dripping over memory & the white paper
outlawing the pumping of our blood

they will drag it like a rock
so that the news of the future

travels no further back
than my father

as his history unravels before him
like the gutted insides of a computer

& everything is hidden
because no-one knows how to live

& the unremembered life will curse us with its silence
singing farewell through shards of pottery

as it disappears beneath the earth
scraping the poetry from our hospitality

& all that I cannot give you
because they have cut out my tongue

# IN PIEROWALL KIRKYARD

With their feet to the rising
& their heads to the setting Sun
the dead of Westray
are the perfect audience
out there on the blue flint of the sea
is a comedy
the green fields & the sliding azure horizon
cannot glinch
out there is the select band of tragedians
whose names are scratched on every stone
making us laugh
ah cloud ah sail ah red keel
this night this green transformer
is singing liberty

# FIRTH MUSIC

The music is blown away on the wind
the music is wrapped up in the wind
I taste the almonds of its melody
I lick the voice of its melody
the fog-symphonies in from the North Sea
May ends June begins the headland disappears
orcas devour seals in the bay
blood flushes the tide
the dorsal fins emerge, submerge
circle & work through the foam & flesh
then are gone & the salt ruckus
is the domain of hysterical herring gulls
half insane on glut & killing

in the memory of sunlight
mackerel flash & bait-ball
then they too vanish beneath the cliff

berserk Arctic skuas gluff razorbills
who may or may not spill their sandeels

blackback gulls allow the air to caress
in updraft the elegance of their wingspan
& all the while the music
the music of the cliff-ledges & the life
& death that is the melody
of these ancient rocks
the melody of touch, of sky, of sea
as language pours through the Pentland Firth
like the blood of seals
the feathers of silence

# BLOOD FOG

June sea-fog
our usual Summer covering
as if sleep were the sea
& Caithness its dreaming place
a democracy of shadows
whose language is blood
this grey dank receding morning
can we forge the gods out of this
a soaked smithage of verse
a salt-hoard of knowledge
far from Persia but not Papigoe
where treeless priests drank alphabets
of cod & herring
to the cack-cacking liturgy of seabirds

2

It rolls in from the North-East over Orkney
smoking the surface of the Pentland Firth
full of noise & nothing
above it all the blue infuriation of the sky
bees hover at the cliff edge
working their way through a brush of seapinks
fulmars appear from beneath the green lip
wing-stiff & subtle they make solid the thermals
to hold the greedy cry of the blackheaded gulls
which Hamlet-like pierces from beyond the fog
will dragon-prows appear
& red & black sails
with Olaf Tryggvason aft the oars
the blood of Christ dripping from his battleaxe?

# ST ANDREW'S DAY

Caithness emerges into the last day of November
Watten loch feeds the night to her trout
the Eastern sky is growing red
& Wick awakens with a salty shout

"Oh here I am Winter
dance right down to my bones
no howling gale or systems failure
can stop the Queen of The Morning as she comes
sailing the sea-roads from Norway
scattering light at the wedding
of these fields & cliffs to history"

Caithness grows like a newly baked loaf
November fades like yesterday's bread
Watten loch is silver now
like the beautiful dream of the dead

# PENTECOST

Black is an intense blue
only seen when the Moon
lets go of the night
or the bottom of the sea
has risen up & spilled
onto the rocks at Dwarick
& the cliffs receive the salt
of the black blessing deep
with a sandstone shiver

Ali Mooner comes to the pier
with his tongue on fire
& infuses Dunnet Bay
undoing Babel as he acquires
the ability to understand
the mighty works of the beginning
before & after the Flood
he sips his green whisky
tasting his favourite danger

Being observed Ali observes
he listens to the black
blue understanding of the sea
which fills his ears
with briny ladders
he climbs into the tide loft
where the understood anchor
their faults & their expression
off he sails in search of a language

# THE MIGHTY ATLANTIC

Surrounded by nothing
you are a god
producing everything
you are a god
mighty Atlantic
joining north to north
south to south
ice to fire
born of earth
the world's
salt drum

Holborn Head
Dunnet Head
two arms to balance
your rolling western swing
sea strath
glen of salt
five thousand terrible tides
your spit
tastes
the lip of the world
with a sea of drum

ah brine angel
deliver now the stagger
of two continents
retrieve for us
the flagstone appetite

of a killer whale
cultivate the kelp-land
of sea-mile & fathom
present to us
the storm-wrecked prayer
of distance to coast

summon your heart
which is a drum
an island of skin
in a percussive firth
to fall among you
is not to drown
but to hear forever
the grinding symphonies
love's cruel geography
kicks us into
ah Atlantic drum


so I prelude you
mighty Atlantic
like blood
like birth
like revenge
we betray you
with our prayers
we besiege you
with our fear
our continent
like a drum

forgive us also
how we banish
your fingerprints
how we abandon ship
in your vast memory
of wave-humans
of how we recognize
everything & nothing
like blind silent dogs
we rummage in the ashes
in the sea-hearth of the planet

our ultimate drum

# BLUE

Blue the firth is blue
lighter in zig zag
as the tides run off Holborn
deeper out to Hoy
& to the east off Dunnet
it is grey like a sermon
melting into the sky white now
inside the darker wave
is the darker blue
like melancholy
it wraps its green eye
against the barnacled June rock
silver the now sea is blue
a plate slid in beside West Murkle
Thurso East a river of slate
terns dive in the bay
the beach is wet from the Sun
& stretches out like a bone
& a man walks across it to time
to catch his blue shadow
& if he only knew it
he could surf to Hoy
there is no wind
bees buzz inside their sleep
& push through the compass of a dandelion
& starlings poke at nothing
& call it their own
upon the green geo funeral cliff
& all the while music

the liquid leaf falling sound of the sea
painting the north
white then blue then blue
yet again blue
the gulls are white grey
one-legged watchers
tip-toeing on seaweed & shipping
blue is their herring gut stare
as islands become the sea
the firth the tide the music the colour
blue all merging fully rising
in the Pentland mouth of the Atlantic
one blue June morning looking for Brazil

# THE ATLANTIC FOREST

A boy stands on a headland
& looks at the islands to the north
the cliffs below him drop into the Pentland Firth
to his left there is the yellow sweep of a bay
beyond that a green coast
out way out beyond all that
is the Atlantic forest
he cannot see it because it is a wide ocean
because it is a big dream inside his small head
there on a sandstone pinnacle
on Scotland's northern coast
because he has been told
he cannot see
but he can see it fine
he can see the timber shore
somewhere in Brazil or Nicaragua
he can see a boy lounging in a tree
looking back

# IN THE ATLANTIC FOREST

Two orange eyes come out of the sky
the illumination of the beyond
bringing it down to here
the black cat of opposition
I am uneasy
nothing is easy to begin
the house is full of Daddy-Long-Legs
clicking & flicking all through the night
phones ring no-one answers
the eyes are staring
night after rainy night
the brutal pores of the state are sweating
burning up empathy
killing people for being alive


2


*For Jean Charles de Menezes 1978 – 2005*


Guns will always fail
history too will fail
has already failed
so Hollywood will make a film
of your short life
just to cheapen it
Sophocles had his chorus sing
"Pity the man who is alive
death is always better"
yet Sophocles lived to be ninety

& was – history thinks – happy
Messiaen saw God in the singing of birds
& made music in their honour
do guns also belong to God?

3

*Blair*

He has never learned what Machiavelli taught
that it is better to be feared than loved
like a timeless Jesuit
it is what makes him deadly
Machiavelli's main concern was fascination
the ins & outs of Florentine power
even his clothes shunned mediocrity
o foggy night
o rowan night
o dowy night
o moon
the deep ocean of the silver air
the honest hopeful heart
will in all seasons prevail

4

The morning started brightly but dulled over
Marx & Calvin were playing poker
both determined to win
I have no privilege so cannot be sceptical
although Montaigne I salute you

big-head feeding Shakespeare
the ice-cream of a philosophy
in the second-best bed of his theatre
telling him to dream of contracts
money stories fame stuff
I watch them all from the front row of the stalls
of my time in rehearsal
hoping for the starlight of purpose
& those glorious eight minutes of travel


5


What can we say of this terrifying tribe?
Sometimes they take one of their number
& leave them hanging from trees
then consume everything around them
& share nothing no matter the need
leaving it to others to pay
what Du Bois called "the wage of whiteness"
I can see we can see they can see
nothing anymore except England America Africa
"the magnificent superstructure" of Postlethwayt
how my heart lifts when I hear her voice
gypsy dancer married to a fool
her skin is black from centuries of Sun
carried off by the devil's breed in ships


6


Galileo told us that Saturn has seven rings
now the press tell us that a bust

travel agent's only retrievable asset was a horse
how a Scottish regiment made a penguin a Colonel
I am on my knees & the foggy full moon
instructs the radio to transmit
crazy German minimalist singing
I am praying to Cronus
to warn him about his son Jupiter
how he is driving an Abrahms tank
how the old gods are not safe
how they are emptying Gaza to fill up the West Bank
all this from a rain-soaked supplicant
on the poor flat threshing floor of reason

7

The plantations stretch across the hills
& the people yet to see the first day
of liberty get only a diet of war films
& musicals disguised as community art
look yonder & you will see
Rilke's terrible angels over Knoydart
& his lovers ripped apart
by the cynical peddlers of circus
& sporting competitions lipped in
by a list of celebrities wishing for
the marching boots of colour
so from this the hills will burn
to expose that crippling thing
the great lie called human nature

8

The rosebay willowherb burns through the long grass
fireweed the nearest to Sun
we have seen this sodden Summer
I watch the wind fan the feathery blood
that pumps through the search
for the ecstatic moment
which joins sensation to experience
the thing that explodes in cities at home
wherever "home" decides to be
or in vast deserts which are so empty
they are worth not counting the dead for
yet we plough on & blood dries quickly
& tragedies are soon forgotten
this way the war drags on until the adverts

9

I have wandered through the Atlantic forest
with Mannon Mhic Lear in my blood
my heart bursting like ferns
from Sun & salt & the atrocity
of a treeless world with the echo
of Narcissus on a chainsaw
transforming Eden into Thanatos
Amazonia & Caledonia
into the dust-cloud cattle ranches of Brazil
where after two years the soil surrenders
to the seduction of the air
which I breathe now hauling

a thousand-year-old pine trunk
from the omphalic black sucrose of a Caithness bog

10

The pale yellow-green crucifixion of the rocket flowers
emboss themselves against the gushing melba
pink symphony of the poppies
in this brief Matisse of a northern Summer
the roots of this Yyggdrasil reach down
to the mono-seasonal steam of the Equator
saying "We are Winter's life-tree"
& the soles of my feet slide an awkward duet
through the clover-wet silage of daisy-grass
as the witnessing wind turns the pages
of the bone-scratched statements
of those who have seen the rainforest burn
they ribbed an inky cross by their name in English
as they filed down from Kildonan to the sea

11

Now the light through the branches pours
golden green whisky from twig to roost
nornlike shaping of breath to step
moving like Ratatosk with the gossip of Summer
from hawk to snake the sky
will fill this foliage to wash the frost
from the bitter tongue of black destruction
with the honey of knowledge tapped from trees
& the two arms of the forest

welcome both the singular Northern Star
& the many-eyed Argus of the South
for here is an ocean-tree like no other
caressing the world with masts & paper
hurting like Yyggdrasil to give us life

12

Forty years ago I ran through the invisible trees
stacked up on Dunnet Beach gleaning melancholy
from the felled pines layered like Kirby grips
to keep the dunes from dancing across the road
smelled the faint green needle-waft
of the vast acres of rolling St Lawrence lumber
& imagined I was skipping over these giant logs
a balaclava of beaver skin folded on my head
& the warming laughter of French brandy
being squeezed from a button accordion
so that I heard it in the Xmas Dunnet dance hall
where we "Stripped The Willow" for a century or two
all this as I held the craggy egg of a pine cone
watching the lost ones of Nova Scotia walk out of the waves

13

The cliffs are bare now the birds have gone
the empty ledges weep the guano white
of an early September westerly hugging ships
close to Holborn Head nose-in
to the angry ruffs in the skirt of the firth
which stretches to the Gulf of Mexico

washing palm-nuts up on Rackwick
Kinlochbervie fish-boxes surprising Bermuda
forces the lucky poets of history
to hang their sea-soaked clothes
on the harbour wall of their achievement
even if that resembles feathers & silence
even if it is reducing like the Atlantic forest
in this St Kilda of vacancy & time

14

Plato had Tirnaeus say that God being good
created the Universe from the incorporeal substance
of ideas & the material elements & mixed them up
& formed the world according to certain geometrics
which resulted in water & trees & us
so we will not sink or float or turn
to myth to be lost or exist in quotations
or lose the dreaming sensation of proportion
which are these waves Tiresias cannot see
these green Athenes swimming
from the boiling tectonic heart of the Atlantic
which feeds the roots of the world's trees
gives sight to the poor down in the blind flood
to see through the hard places to the stars

# CODA

In Caledon the bards shaped their songs
from an alphabet of trees
now a cauldron of storms
shapes our coasts with the revenge of carbon
which lay in bogs for millennia
& roofed the people against Winter
was burned to ensure the rule of law
that arrogant set of prejudices
which wipes its rank across the map
from the Uists to New Orleans
but carbon is the still centre of the Atlantic lung
raising hotels & casinos as it throws the dollar
into the high branches of decline
when the last leaf falls a new forest grows

# Poetry from Two Ravens Press

## Castings
### Mandy Haggith

A new collection of poems by Mandy Haggith, whose writing reflects her love for the land and her concern for the environment – not just in the North-West Highlands where she now lives on a woodland croft, but also in her travels around the world.

*'The poetry here shows real clarity of eye marking the dialogues of nature in a place, be that place the lonely Scottish crofting area that is home, or the course of the River Kelvin through the Lowlands, or a Russian forest.'* **Tom Leonard**

*'Outstanding originality and quality. Impressive for its sharpness, sympathy and decisiveness...'* **Alan Riach**

£8.99. ISBN 978-1-906120-01-6. Published April 2007.

## Leaving the Nest
### Dorothy Baird

A collection of poetry by Dorothy Baird that represents a woman's journey into adulthood, through childbirth and motherhood and then on, as her children grow up and she passes into menopause and beyond.

*'These pieces are the outpouring of a remarkable talent...They are unobtrusively urgent, unashamed, and alive with longing lingering thoughts and feelings, with intensely personal experiences which Dorothy Baird has triumphantly universalised...In an increasingly ugly and unpredictable world, these poems are a reminder and an example of just how beautiful life can be.'* **Christopher Rush**

£8.99. ISBN 978-1-906120-06-1. Published July 2007.

## The Zig Zag Woman
### Maggie Sawkins

A first collection of poetry by Maggie Sawkins.

*'Maggie Sawkins draws brilliantly on extended metaphor and the surreal to explore painful relationships, mental illness and problematic situations. She writes both from personal experience and beyond it. Her inventive and highly individual voice is always authentic. The taut writing carries emotional weight and sends that shiver up my spine which tells me I am reading real poetry. This is a very exciting first collection.'* **Myra Schneider**

£8.99. ISBN 978-1-906120-08-5. Published September 2007.

# In a Room Darkened
## Kevin Williamson

A first poetry collection by the founder, publisher and editor of the renowned underground literary magazine *Rebel Inc.*

'...*with a cast including Taggart, Karl Marx, Walt Disney, John Coltrane, Robert the Bruce, Pinocchio, Jesus, Norman MacCaig and Grandmaster Flash, it is a genuine pleasure to watch him swither.*'
**Marc Horne, Scotland on Sunday**

£8.99. ISBN 978-1-906120-07-8. Published October 2007

# Running With a Snow Leopard
## Pamela Beasant

A first collection by Orkney poet and George Mackay Brown Fellow Pamela Beasant.

'...*breathtakingly evocative detail...unabashed spontaneity – and sheer musicality.*' **Stewart Conn, former Edinburgh Makar**

£8.99. ISBN 978-1-906120-14-6. Published January 2008

# In The Hanging Valley
## Yvonne Gray

A collection of poetry by writer and musician Yvonne Gray.

'*Yvonne Gray's poems breathe with the air of Orkney. She is a musician as well as a poet, and one can detect the musician's ear in her writing. Her poems stitch images into a fabric: one rich and textured but at the same time light and unshowy. They address the changing landscapes of a dear place, its rich history and wildlife. They pay homage to artists and musicians, to people of the past as well as those of present. With words she paints the picture, the music.*'
**Christine De Luca**

£8.99. ISBN 978-1-906120-19-1. Published March 2008

---

For more information on these and other titles, and for book extracts and author interviews, see our website.

**Titles are available P&P-free, direct from the publisher at**
## www.tworavenspress.com